Marketplace

An International Celebration of Culture and Commerce

Photographs and Text
by

Matthew Cull

Life's Passion Publishing

Photographs from China, Tibet, Nepal, India, Pakistan, Myanmar, Thailand, Japan, Ecuador, Peru, Tanzania

To the beauty, complexity, solace, joy, life and force of nature

Flower stall, Ayacucho, Peru

The old style marketplace is a heady brew. Streets and alleys lined with stalls whose products have erupted onto the pavement leaving slender passages between goods. Town squares a maze of stalls and products with folks picking their way around a miriad of choices displayed in artistic arrangements. Wafting aromas of spices, animals, flowers or over-ripe vegetables. Voices of folks in casual conversation, bargaining in negotiations, or arguing in dispute. The squeal of a pig being dragged to a new home, the clucking of chickens, the chirps of chicks, a fight between dogs over scraps. Goods provide life and texture in a dazzling array of color. Fruits, nuts, vegetables and spices in conical piles; flowers in tight bunches; bolts of fabric piled from floor to ceiling; handicrafts draped from wires and hangers; restaurant stalls prepare traditional receipes to a hungry crowd; idle stall owners wait patiently for the next customer; buyers wander from stall to stall inspecting the goods and bargaining for the best price. Hand made and hand grown goods intermingle with machine made western style products. Its all part of the sensory joy of the marketplace.

The supermarket has been the death of the marketplace. Sanitized high volume consumerism with one stop shop -

convenience put an end to the local vendor selling a small range of colorful products artfully arranged. Western orderliness and need for protection from the elements put the goods and the sellers inside and out of sight with goods clinically displayed on shelves, the product hidden behind multiple layers of packaging with graphics rather than product being the lure. Ease won out over color, character and culture. Economies of scale pushed the small vendor into history. The marketplace, was once in our culture, and is still in many others, the social and economic hub of community and society. Daily or weekly markets drew villages and townsfolk from the surrounding landscape. Folks came with their own products to sell and returned home with goods their family or community needed. The market was a focus of income, commerce, socialization, and a venue and means for society to flourish, for folks to bond, mix and exchange ideas on a personal level. Much of that has been lost in a modern society that demands efficiency over personality, sanitization over experience, and uniformity over individuality. The life and vitality of the market has faded into a cultural monotony indistinguishable from one land, one people to another. This book shows that in spite of the trend towards cultural homogenization, in many regions of the world the market is still alive and bursting with color, life, products and mystery.

Sweet store, Calcutta, India

Restaurant stall, Nyuangschwe, Myanmar

刚到
新西瓜
3毛

Xian, Shaanxi province, China

Xian, Shaanxi province, China

Spices, Rawalpindi, Pakistan

Fabric to make shalwar kameez for men, the national clothing of Pakistan

Traditional dress for Peruvian women, displayed in Huanta

Handicraft stall, Saquisili, Ecuador

Flowers are used for
celebrations and festivals,
Kathmandu, Nepal

Mask stall, Kathmandu,
Nepal

Cooked chicken to go, Kashgar, Xinjiang province, China

Restaurant, Kashgar, China

Wall hangings, Lhasa, Tibet

Yak butter stall, Lhasa, Tibet

Store in a covered market,
Kyoto, Japan

18

Try before you buy, Takayam
Japan

Dali, Yunnan province, China

Dali, Yunnan province, China

Kalaw, Myanmar

Kalaw, Myanmar

23

Nang Rong, Thailand

Krabi, Thailand

Calcutta, India

paring a vegetable dish, Calcutta, India

Bird cage store, Rawalpindi,
Pakistan

The bicycle of choice for most of Asia, Rawalpindi, Pakistan

Roadside vegetable vendor between Arusha and Moshi, Tanzania

Lushoto, Tanzania

Kathmandu, Nepal

Kathmandu, Nepal

Jauja, Peru

Kunming, Yunnan province, China

康熙皇帝

仁宗嘉慶皇帝

Beijing, China

Kalaw, Myanmar

Nyuangschwe, Myanmar

Kashgar, Xinjiang province, China

Xian, Shaanxi province, China

Flute vendor, Kathmandu,
Nepal

42

Figurine vendor, Kathmandu, Nepal

Stalls sell decorations for important celebrations, Rawalpindi, Pakistan

Grain merchant, Rawalpindi, Pakistan

Fresh fruit juice vendor, Rawalpindi, Pakistan

Lijiang, Yunnan Province, China

CONDIMENTOS EN GRAL.   CONDI

Copacabana, Bolivia

Chil

Cheroots, the national smoke of Myanmar

Floor mats, Nyuangschwe, Myanmar

Yuanmou, Yunnan province, China

Flower stall on a bicycle, Kunming,
Yunnan province, China

Riobamba, Ecuador

Cuenca, Ecuador

Selling miracle cures, Rawalpindi, Pakistan

Newspaper rack, Rawalpindi, Pakistan

Mandarin distribution center,
Calcutta, India

Disposable clay cups for street
sold tea, Calcutta, India

Life forms on a stick at an outdoor restaurant market, Beijing China

Yuanmou, Yunnan province, China

Kalaw, Myanmar

Nyuangschwe, Myanmar

Banos, Ecuador

Alausi, Ecuador

Lijiang, Yunnan province, China

Kunming, Yunnan province, China

Shawl vendor, Kathmandu, Nepal

Chappati and curry, Lahore, Pakistan

Florist, Calcutta, India

Implements of chivalry, Pushkar, Rajasthan, India

Fabric vendor in a labyrinth of covered alleys, Lahore, Pakistan

Rawalpindi, Pakistan

Before, Otavalo animal ma

After, Otavalo, Ecuador

Nyuangschwe, Myanmar

Nyuangschwe, Myanmar

Inspecting cuy, guinea pigs, a delicacy in Ecu

Saquilsili, Ecuador

Kashgar, Xinjiang province, China

Kashgar, Xinjiang Province, China

Pokhara, Nepal

Kathmandu, Nepal

Endangered species become warm hats, Kashgar, Xinjiang province, China

imported from Turkey, Kashgar, Xinjiang province, China

Alausí, Ecuador

Otavalo, Ecuador

Xian, Shaanxi province, China

Tibetan Buddhist monks stock up in Xiahe, Gansu province, China

Yangon, Myanmar

Bago, Myanmar

Kunming, Yunnan province, China

Marketplace An International Celebration of Culture and Commerce

First Edition: March 2012

ISBN: 978-0-9850790-5-5

Library of Congress Control Number: 2012901818

Text by Matthew Cull
Photography by Matthew Cull
Book design by Matthew Cull

To purchase additional copies contact:

Many of the photographs in this book are available as fine art prints. Contact:

Life's Passion Publishing
P.O. Box 2962
Vail, Colorado, 81658
matthewcull@me.com

www.matthewjkcull.com

Printed in USA by Four Colour Print Group

Other Titles in the International Celebration of Culture Series

Kids, An International Celebration of Culture and Children

Women, An International Celebration of Culture and Gender

Men, An International Celebration of Culture and Gender

Parent and Child, An International Celebration of Culture and Family

Faith, An International Celebration of Culture and Belief